Dana Facaros and
Michael Pauls

SOUTH OF FRANCE

'a delicious southern world of
crystalline rock, olive trees and
uncanny sunlight'

CADOGANguides

Contents

About the authors

Dana Facaros and **Michael Pauls** have written over 30 books for Cadogan Guides. They have lived all over Europe, and are currently ensconced in an old farmhouse in south-west France.

About the updaters

Robin Pridy splits her time between Brighton, England, and western Canada. She writes on arts and travel for newspapers and magazines, and has edited a number of Cadogan Guides.

Kate Read and her husband left the pressures of London for the peace of a farm-house in southwest France, and have lived there for the past 11 years with their two sons. Kate runs a holiday letting service in the region and is currently writing a cookery book.

Cadogan Guides
Highlands House, 165 The Broadway,
London SW19 1NE
info.cadogan@virgin.net
www.cadoganguides.com

The Globe Pequot Press
246 Goose Lane, PO Box 480, Guilford,
Connecticut 06437–0480

Copyright © Dana Facaros and Michael Pauls
    1992, 1994, 1997, 1999, 2001, 2003

Cover and photo essay design by Kicca Tommasi
Book design by Andrew Barker
Cover photographs: © Jon Arnold,
    © John Ferro Sims
Maps © Cadogan Guides,
    drawn by Map Creation Ltd.
Managing editor: Christine Stroyan
Editor: Lindsay Porter
Art direction: Sarah Rianhard-Gardner
Proofreading: Molly Perham
Indexing: Isobel McLean
Production: Navigator Guides Ltd

Printed in Italy by Legoprint
A catalogue record for this book is available
    from the British Library
ISBN 1-86011-883-6

The author and publishers have made every effort to ensure the accuracy of the information in this book at the time of going to press. However, they cannot accept any responsibility for any loss, injury or inconvenience resulting from the use of information contained in this guide.

Please help us to keep this guide up to date. We have done our best to ensure that the information in this guide is correct at the time of going to press. But places and facilities are constantly changing, and standards and prices in hotels and restaurants fluctuate. We would be delighted to receive any comments concerning existing entries or omissions. Authors of the best letters will receive a copy of the Cadogan Guide of their choice.

a photo essay

Esterel coastline  valley in the
Alpes-Maritimes

Vieux Port, Marseille  cabin in the Camargue
Côtes-de-Provence
vineyard
vineyards, Vaucluse

view from
Jardin Exotique, Eze
Roussillon  cork oaks
the ruins of Glanum,
St-Rémy-de-Provence

Place Masséna, Nice
Golfe-Juan  Fayence

L'Escarène  Avignon

Albi Tarn, Languedoc  Alpes-Maritimes

the Toulourenc Valley
below Mont Ventoux